MUMMIES, TOMBS, AND TREASURE

Secrets of Ancient Egypt

by Lila Perl

Drawings by Erika Weihs

Illustrated with photographs

Clarion Books

New York

For
ABDULWAHĀB ALY HEGAZY
. . . who lit the way

Clarion Books
a Houghton Mifflin Company imprint
215 Park Avenue South, New York, NY 10003
Text copyright © 1987 by Lila Perl
Drawings copyright © 1987 by Erika Weihs
Printed in the USA

Library of Congress Cataloging-in-Publication Data
Perl, Lila.
Mummies, tombs, and treasure.

Bibliography: p. 113
Includes index.
Summary: Text and photographs examine the mummies
and tombs of ancient Egypt.
1. Mummies—Egypt—Pictorial works—Juvenile
literature. 2. Tombs—Egypt—Pictorial works—
Juvenile literature. 3. Egypt—Antiquities—
Pictorial works—Juvenile literature. [1. Mummies—
Egypt. 2. Tombs—Egypt. 3. Egypt—Antiquities]
I. Title.
DT62.M7P49 1987   932   86-17646
ISBN 0-89919-407-9   PA ISBN 0-395-54796-2

3456789-B-96 95 94

MUMMIES, TOMBS, AND TREASURE

Other Clarion Books by Lila Perl

Blue Monday and Friday the Thirteenth
The Stories Behind the Days of the Week

Candles, Cakes, and Donkey Tails
Birthday Symbols and Celebrations

Piñatas and Paper Flowers
Piñatas y flores de papel
Holidays of the Americas in English and Spanish

Junk Food, Fast Food, Health Food
What America Eats and Why

Hunter's Stew and Hangtown Fry
What Pioneer America Ate and Why

Slumps, Grunts, and Snickerdoodles
What Colonial America Ate and Why

The Hamburger Book
All About Hamburgers and Hamburger Cookery

Contents

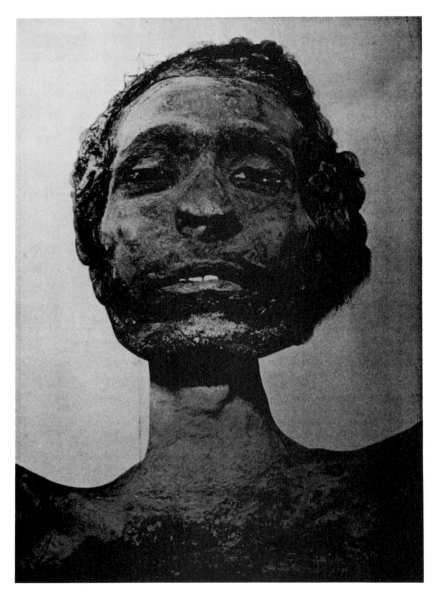

The 3000-year-old mummy of an ancient Egyptian priest

1

The First Egyptian Mummies

What is a mummy, and why do we find mummies so fascinating? We've all heard of old-time horror movies with names like *The Mummy's Hand*, *The Mummy's Ghost*, and *The Mummy's Tomb*. And then there is "the mummy's curse." Even today there are people who believe that anyone who has ever gone near a mummy will meet with sudden misfortune.

Yet a mummy is nothing more than a dead body, either human or animal. Perhaps the reason mummies fill some of us with fear and fire up our imaginations is that they are so lifelike. Many Egyptian mummies are thousands of years old. But they still have their hair, their fingernails and toenails, and even their eyelashes. Their flesh and their features are well preserved. In looking at photographs taken when these mummies were discovered, in recent times, we can tell them apart and recognize their faces.

A mummy, of course, is a dead body that has been

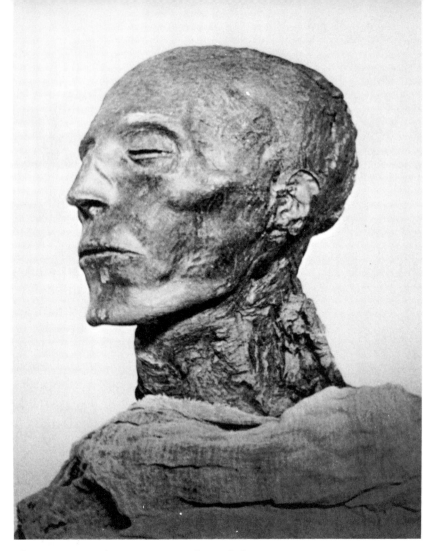

The mummy of King Seti I, who ruled Egypt 3,300 years ago

preserved — either accidentally by nature or on purpose by humans. Without preservation, dead animal matter usually decays very quickly. This is true of plant matter, too. A dead bird or cat, a piece of rotting fruit, can show us some of the stages of decay. Decay is caused by bacteria. These microscopic organisms break down the tissues of once-living things, returning them to nature in other forms.

But sometimes nature springs a surprise or two on us. One such surprise took place long ago in the vast North African desert country of Egypt. Before the beginning of recorded history — perhaps seven or eight thousand years ago — people began to settle on the banks of the Nile River, which runs through the Egyptian desert. The ribbons of well-watered land that bordered the Nile provided precious soil for growing food crops. So, in selecting a place to bury their dead, the Egyptian farming people avoided the river shore. They chose instead the hot, barren sands that lay beyond it.

The people dug small shallow graves. Usually they buried their dead in a crouched position. They placed them on their sides with their knees drawn up to their chests. That way their bodies took up as little space as possible.

The Egyptians hoped that in some magical way the dead were not really dead. Perhaps their spirits lay beneath the sand along with their limp, unclothed bodies. Perhaps a spirit might wish to eat or drink just as the living did. So the families of the dead included some clay pots of food and jars of water in the shallow pit graves. And sometimes they added a man's favorite tool or spear of sharpened stone, a woman's beads of shell or bone, or a child's toy.

Then the family covered the grave with sand and piled some rocks on top of it. The rocks helped to mark the grave. They also made it difficult for jackals and other wild animals of the desert to reach the body inside it.

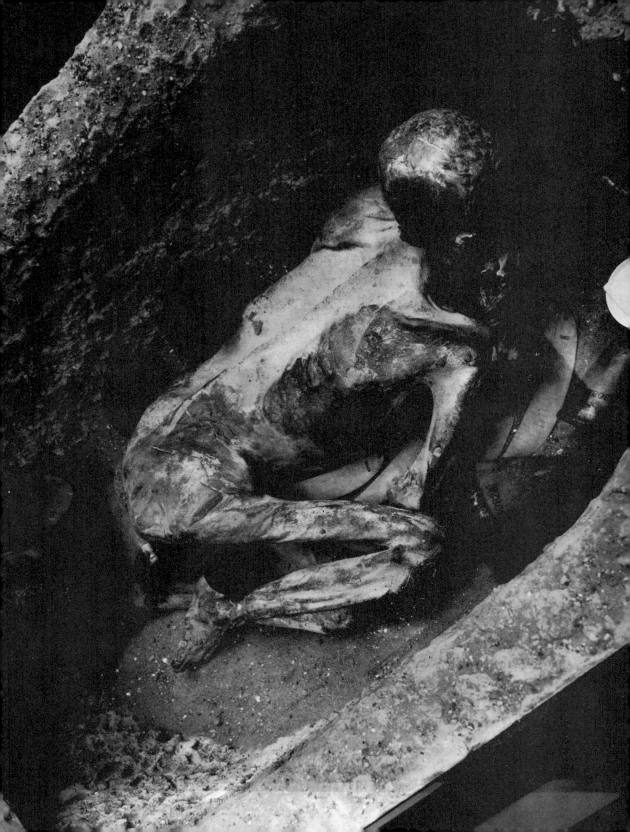

The hot dry sand of the shallow unlined graves did an amazing thing: it preserved the bodies of the early Egyptians wonderfully well. Moisture helps bacteria in bringing about decay. And the human body contains about seventy-five percent water. By rapidly absorbing the body's moisture, the hot sand acted as a natural preservative. The skin and other organs dried instead of decaying, and the first Egyptian mummies were born!

Similar accidents of nature have taken place in other parts of the world. But the early Egyptians had no way of knowing about those.

We know today, for example, that bodies can be naturally preserved by dry cold as well as by dry heat. In Siberia in northern Asia, woolly mammoths — huge prehistoric animals that resembled hairy elephants — have been found well preserved in ice. Their mummified bodies are at least ten thousand years old, for that is when the last of the mammoths died out.

Dry cold has also preserved the bodies of the Incas of Peru. The people of that far-reaching Indian empire lived in the high Andes Mountains of South America. Until they were conquered by Spanish explorers about five hundred years ago, they placed their dead in rock shelters. They arranged the bodies in a sitting position with knees drawn up, and bound them into bundles, wrapped in cloth, grass, and fur. In the dry, crisp mountain air, the Inca dead were soon transformed into mummies.

The early Egyptians must have been pleased when they somehow discovered the naturally mummified bodies of their dead. Soon they looked for ways to improve their graves. They lined the burial pits with straw

A naturally preserved mummy, with fingernails, toenails, and a few locks of reddish hair, found in a shallow desert grave

matting or with animal skins. And, as time went on, they added a crude floor and walls of sun-dried bricks. The bricks were made of chopped straw and mud, and were molded by hand. Some burial chambers even had ceilings of rough wooden beams. Such graves were costly because wood was very scarce in Egypt, a land with few trees.

The Nile farmers were becoming more prosperous, though. Each year when the river flooded its banks, it deposited a rich layer of mud and renewed the fertility of the soil. The farmers dug a network of irrigation ditches. This brought water into their fields so that there would be enough moisture throughout the growing season. Rain almost never fell in the Egyptian desert.

As the population living along the Nile grew, life became less simple. Village governments had to be formed to keep careful records of the lush farmland known as the "black land." (The desert, by contrast, was called the "red land.") The village officials measured property boundaries, oversaw the digging of irrigation canals, noted the amount of grain that was stored from each year's harvest, and started collecting taxes from the Nile villagers. Soon the villages were organized into bigger regions, or provinces, and finally into two kingdoms — Upper Egypt and Lower Egypt.

Then, about five thousand years ago, all of Egypt came under the rule of a single king. He was known as the "lord of the two lands." The year in which Upper Egypt and Lower Egypt were united was about 3100 B.C., and the name of the first king was Menes (MEN-eez).

It is always confusing to learn that Upper Egypt is

really the southern part of the country and Lower Egypt the northern part. This is because the Nile River flows from south to north, carrying the waters of melting snows and jungle rains from the mountains and forests of central Africa. So Upper Egypt is "upriver" from Lower Egypt.

Map of Egypt today. Cities and sites of ancient Egypt are in italics.

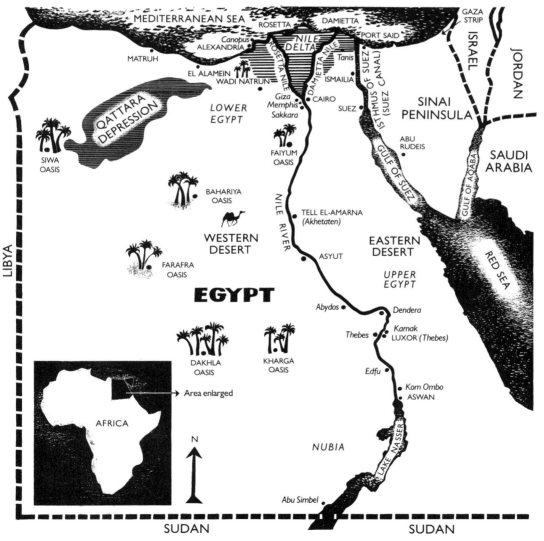

UPPER EGYPT   LOWER EGYPT   DOUBLE CROWN

The crown of Upper Egypt, the crown of Lower Egypt, and the double crown of the "two lands"

The new king wore an interesting crown. It combined the old pear-shaped white crown of Upper Egypt and the boxy red crown of Lower Egypt, one set atop the other. This headdress was known as the "double crown." It was an important symbol of the joining of the two parts of the country.

Now that Egypt had become a great kingdom, what was going to happen to its powerful ruler when he died? He certainly could not be buried naked in a shallow desert grave, not even one that was lined with brick and roofed with wood. A great king needed a proper coffin of wood or even stone.

So, while commoners continued to be buried in the old way, kings and their queens, and other nobles were

A wooden statue of an Egyptian king wearing the short white kilt and the white crown of Upper Egypt

more carefully prepared for burial. Instead of being left unclothed, their bodies were wrapped in strips of linen, the same cloth that Egyptians wore throughout their lives. Linen was woven from flax, which was grown along the Nile. Cotton was unknown in Egypt at the time, and wool was too coarse, itchy, and hot. Many people considered it "unclean."

But, unlike the short white linen kilt worn by men or the long, close-fitting linen dress worn by women, the clothing of the dead consisted of tightly wound bandages. And to protect the body even further, the Egyptians poured warm resin over the layers of bandages until they were well soaked. Resin was an oily, sticky extract that came from certain plants. Because it did not dissolve in water and hardened to a varnish-like finish, the Egyptians figured it would keep the body dry.

Then they placed the body in a tightly closed coffin and buried it deeper than the ordinary pit grave. Because the early kings and queens were laid to rest with valuable jewelry and other treasures, the Egyptians wanted to be sure that the grave goods would be safe from both animals and humans.

But the new royal burials turned out to be a horrible mistake. Locked into their layers of bandages and sealed in their thick-walled coffins, the bodies of the rulers rapidly decayed from within. The hot, dry sand that would have mummified them was shut out.

The Egyptians learned of this when grave robbers tunneled deep beneath the desert sands and broke open the coffins to steal the royal treasures. All that remained inside the stiff coating of bandages was a heap of bones.

There was no mummy, no likeness of the dead person at all!

Clearly, the Egyptians had to find a better way of making mummies. Nature had shown them one way to do it. But they wanted grander burials, more secure and impressive tombs. Above all they wanted mummies that were as well preserved, or even better, than those that were buried directly in the sand.

The Egyptians of the newly formed kingdom would have to find some other method for transforming their dead into lifelike and long-lasting mummies.

Khnum, the Egyptian god with the head of a ram, who created people on his potter's wheel

2
Why the Egyptians Made Mummies

Why did the Egyptians want to make mummies in the first place? Very likely it was because of their strong belief in the magical power of images.

They believed that, in addition to a body, every person had a soul or spirit that would live on after death. The spirit could do many things. It could eat, drink, move about, and enjoy the same pleasures as when the body had been alive. But, in order to do these things, the spirit had to have a recognizable body to dwell in.

If the person's image — the body — was destroyed, the spirit might not be able to live on after death. So preserving the body was very important.

Among the ancient Egyptians, the soul or spirit took several forms. The two that were most common were the *ka* and the *ba*.

The *ka* was a person's double, an unseen twin. The Egyptians believed that all people and their *ka*s were created by a god named Khnum (KNOOM). Khnum was

King Tutankhamen (center), with his ka *just behind him, embracing Osiris, the god of the dead*

said to make the newborn out of clay, on his potter's wheel. Like many Egyptian gods and goddesses, Khnum had the body of a human and the head of an animal — in this case, a ram.

The *ka* lived in the body until death. Once the person died, the *ka* too would die unless it was provided with a very exact image of the dead person. Sometimes a statue would serve to house the *ka*, but a lifelike mummy was best.

The *ka* also needed food in order to survive. When the Egyptian villagers left jars of grains and water in the shallow sand graves of their dead, they were feeding the *ka*. Later, the food offerings in Egyptian tombs became much more lavish.

The *ba* was another form of the dead person's spirit.

Unlike the *ka*, which stayed in the tomb with the mummy, the *ba* was able to leave. It was said to be able to take any shape it liked. But it was usually shown as a small bird with a human head that resembled that of the dead person.

The *ba* could fly out of the tomb, magically passing through walls of solid rock or through deep shafts packed with rough broken stones. But it always returned to the tomb at night, sometimes bearing a small, lighted candle. Like the *ka*, the *ba* had to be able to find and recognize the body to which it belonged. Without a mummy, there would be no *ka* and no *ba*. There would be no

The ba *bird, a form of the dead person's spirit, hovering over the mummy*

afterlife. Death would be final and complete, a fate that the Egyptians could not accept.

Why were the Egyptians so eager for an afterlife? One reason may have been that life along the Nile was so peaceful and pleasant that they wanted it to continue after death. The Nile dwellers were protected from invading armies by the desert that lay to the east and west of the river, the rocky Nile waterfalls to the south, and the sea to the north. The land itself was warm and sunny, and the fields were fruitful. The farmers worked hard, of course. But they were rewarded with the simple necessities of life. The very world in which the afterlife of the farming people was said to take place lay beneath the desert sands and parallel to the life-giving Nile River.

After Egypt became a great kingdom, the afterlife became even more important. Naturally, a king's afterlife was far different from that of a commoner. It was as rich and luxury-filled as his life on earth, for the king was believed to be an earthly god. And when he died he became a heavenly god who would see to the well-being of his people for ever and ever. He would also be able to seek favor with the many other gods in whom the Egyptians believed.

But none of this could happen unless the king's *ka* survived. And his *ka* could not survive unless his mummy was magnificently prepared to last until the very end of time.

Who were the gods that were so important to the Egyptians? Some of them were gods of nature. They helped to explain the mysteries of why the sun rose each morning and why the Nile River flooded and enriched its banks each year.

*The falcon-headed sun god, Ra, crowned with the disk of the sun
and holding an ankh, the Egyptian symbol for life*

The sun god was called Ra. He was sometimes shown
as having a human body and the head of a falcon crowned
with a disk that represented the sun. The Nile god
(sometimes there were two) was Hapi. He was a human-
headed god with a fleshy chest and belly representing the
bountiful food that the river brought forth. Often, water
lily and papyrus reeds were shown sprouting from his

Two carvings of the fleshy-bodied Nile god, Hapi

head. These plants grew in the river shallows — the water lily in Upper Egypt and the papyrus in Lower Egypt.

Offering daily prayers to Ra and Hapi helped to assure the Egyptians that the sun's warmth and the river's floodwaters would never fail them.

Other gods and goddesses were in charge of love and beauty, of childbirth, of music and dancing, of truth and justice, of arts and crafts, and even of writing. But, of all the Egyptian gods, the ones that were connected with death and the afterlife were the most numerous. Chief among them was Osiris (Oh-SI-ris).

The Egyptians believed that once, long ago, Osiris had been a king of Lower Egypt who was loved by everyone except his jealous brother Set. Set decided to murder

The god of writing, Thoth. He had the head of an ibis, a long-billed, long-legged wading bird of the Nile.

Osiris. So he asked him to a banquet at which all the guests were invited to take turns lying down in a beautiful lidded box to see which one fitted it best. As soon as Osiris climbed into the box and lay down, Set slammed the lid shut. He then cast the box into the Nile, from where it floated into the sea.

Isis (I-sis), the wife of Osiris, went in search of her husband's murdered body. She found it at last in a city on the shore of Asia, in what is now the country of Lebanon. The box had become tangled in the branches of a young tree. It was rescued from the sea because it was lifted higher and higher as the tree grew.

But when Isis returned to Egypt with the body of her husband, the evil Set once again stole Osiris away. This time he cut Osiris's body into fourteen pieces and scattered them all over Egypt. Patiently, with the help of her sister, Nephthys (NEF-this), Isis searched until she found each of the pieces. Magically, the body of Osiris became whole again. From then on, however, he was the god of the dead, and especially of the dead kings of Egypt.

Pictures of Osiris always show him as a wrapped mummy, his legs bandaged together. He wears the false beard that the living Egyptian kings wore at official ceremonies. Often he holds a curved shepherd's crook in one hand, and in the other, a flail — a stick with a loose strap at one end that is used for beating. The crook and the flail were the symbols of the all-powerful Egyptian kings. The crook tells us that the king cared for his people as a shepherd does for his sheep. But the flail is a reminder that he also punished them for wrongdoing.

As the god of the dead, Osiris was also the god of the

Osiris, the Egyptian god of the dead, and his wife, Isis

afterlife. When an Egyptian ruler died, he was said to have "joined" Osiris. Often the king himself would be painted on the wall of his tomb as Osiris, in the form of a mummy. The bandaging of the king's mummy may even have been a symbol of the magical putting together again of the fourteen pieces of the body of Osiris.

The other members of Osiris's family were also connected with the protection of the dead. Isis and her sister Nephthys were often carved or painted on mummy cases and tomb walls wearing large sheltering wings. Isis was also the goddess of wifehood and motherhood, for after Osiris had been murdered she had given birth to their son, Horus.

Horus, when grown, had killed his wicked uncle Set and regained the throne of Egypt. But in the battle with Set, Horus was said to have lost his left eye. Like the sheltering wings of Isis, the eye of Horus was often painted on coffins to enable the dead to "see again."

Horus usually took the form of a falcon-headed god wearing the double crown of Egypt. Set, on the other hand, was pictured as an odd-looking donkeylike animal. The evil Set was the god of the desert, or "red land." The fierce sandstorms that sometimes blew from the west and ruined the Nile crops were blamed on him.

Lastly, there was a god of mummification whose name was Anubis (Ah-NYOO-bis). Anubis had a human body with the head of a jackal. He was said to be the son of Nephthys, and it was his job to prepare the bodies of the dead to be received by Osiris.

Did the Egyptians decide to make royal mummies because they believed in the god Osiris? Or did they invent

Horus, the son of Isis and Osiris, and the magical symbol of the eye of Horus, with a design of falling tears beneath it

the legend of Osiris as an excuse for the elaborate burials they began to give their kings? It's hard to tell because the Egyptian kings and the Egyptian gods were so strongly linked.

Egyptian royalty patterned itself after the gods. The gods, for example, were closely related. Isis was not only the wife of Osiris; she was also his sister. So, to keep the royal family's bloodline pure, a king might marry his sister, half-sister, or cousin. He often took other wives as well. But the first wife remained the "great wife," and whenever possible her son inherited the throne.

An Egyptian ruling line related by blood was known as a dynasty. Most historians agree that ancient Egypt had thirty dynasties spanning nearly three thousand years of its history. But few agree on the exact year when each dynasty began and ended.

One reason for this problem is that the Egyptians themselves did not number the years one after the other. Each time a new king came to the throne, they simply called the first year of his reign the Year I.

Historians have also divided the Egyptian dynasties into groups to make it easier for us to find our way through the long stretch of three thousand years. During that time there were periods of great stability, wealth, and power known as the Old Kingdom, the Middle Kingdom, and the New Kingdom. And there were weaker years in between, known as Intermediate Periods, when the office of the king was challenged by power-seeking priests and governors and by would-be conquerors from outside Egypt.

But, like the smooth-flowing Nile itself, life in Egypt

Anubis, the jackal-headed god of mummification

Dynasties of Ancient Egypt

Dynasty	Approximate Dates, B.C.	Name of Period	Important Rulers Mentioned in Text
1st and 2nd	3100–2700	Early Dynastic	*1st Dynasty* Menes; also known as Narmer
3rd to 6th	2700–2200	Old Kingdom	*3rd Dynasty* Zoser *4th Dynasty* Sneferu Khufu [Cheops] Khafre [Chephren] Menkaure [Mycerinus]
7th to 10th	2200–2050	First Intermediate	
11th and 12th	2050–1800	Middle Kingdom	
13th to 17th	1800–1570	Second Intermediate	
18th to 20th	1570–1085	New Kingdom *18th Dynasty* Ahmose Amenhotep I [Amenophis] Thutmose I [Thutmosis; Tuthmosis] Thutmose II Hatshepsut Thutmose III Amenhotep II Thutmose IV Amenhotep III Akhenaten; also known as Amenhotep IV Tutankhamen	*19th Dynasty* Ramses I Seti I Ramses II *20th Dynasty* Ramses III Ramses IV Ramses V Ramses VI
21st to 25th	1085–700	Third Intermediate	
26th to 30th	700–332	Late Dynastic	
	332–30	Greek	Alexander the Great Ptolemy I to XIV Cleopatra
	30 B.C.	Roman conquest	
	A.D. 640	Moslem conquest	

Note: Names in brackets are Greek versions of Egyptian names.

swept forward. And as death followed life, so the preparation for the afterlife followed death.

For, by the time of the Fourth Dynasty, around 2500 B.C., the Egyptians found what they had been searching for — a much better way to make mummies than ever before. Here at last, they believed, was a way to give all their kings of all the dynasties to come an afterlife. Here was a way for the rulers of Egypt to join the god Osiris and to cheat death forever.

The long-lasting mummy of Queen Notmit of the 21st Dynasty, wearing an elaborate wig

3

How a Mummy Was Made

Making long-lasting mummies turned out to be not so difficult after all. In fact, the Egyptians probably wondered why they hadn't discovered the secret earlier. They simply set about improving on nature by artificially drying out the bodies of the dead *before* burial.

There were, of course, a number of problems to overcome. The first had to do with the moist insides of the body. Those parts were the most likely to cause decay. So the Egyptians decided that the body cavity of the newly dead person would have to be opened up and that the stomach, the intestines, the liver, and the lungs would have to be removed. In a later period of dynastic history, other organs of the body were removed as well.

At first the Egyptians probably shrank from cutting a large gash in the abdomen of their royal dead with a knife of sharpened stone or rock glass. (The Egyptians did not have iron for cutting tools.) But after a while they must have come to realize that this was a small price to pay for the preservation of the body.

It was also decided that the body parts that were removed should not be thrown away. After thorough drying out, each organ — stomach, intestines, liver, and lungs — would be placed in a separate container of wood, pottery, or stone, to be preserved in the tomb forever along with the mummy. As long as the mummy and its insides were protected against decay, the Egyptians believed that all the body parts would be magically reunited in the afterlife, exactly as in the story of Osiris.

As far as we know, the first royal Egyptian to have her body treated in this way was a queen of the Fourth Dynasty named Hetepheres (Het-eh-FAIR-eez). She was the mother of King Khufu, the builder of the world-famous Great Pyramid. The Greek name for this king is Cheops (KEE-opps).

When the tomb of Queen Hetepheres was discovered in 1925, her mummy was missing as a result of a robbery that had taken place soon after her burial. But a chest made of a fine white stone called alabaster was found. It was divided into four compartments that still contained the remains of her stomach and other organs, nearly forty-five hundred years after her death.

In later times in ancient Egypt, it became the custom to put each organ into a separate jar called a canopic (ka-NAH-pik) jar. The word *canopic* comes from the ancient city of Canopus in northern Egypt where Osiris was worshipped in the form of a vase topped with a head.

At the time of the Middle Kingdom, it was usual for each of the four canopic jars to be topped with a carving

Canopic jars with stoppers representing the four sons of Horus: Duamutef, Qebsenuef, Imseti, and Hapi

of a human head. But during the New Kingdom, canopic jar stoppers began to be fashioned after the four sons of Horus.

Each son was believed to protect a different organ. Duamutef, who had the head of a jackal, protected the jar containing the stomach. Qebsenuef, who had the head of a falcon, watched over the intestines. Imseti, a human-headed son of Horus, was in charge of the liver, while the baboon-headed Hapi oversaw the lungs.

As if this sacred guarding of the mummified organs weren't enough, each son of Horus was protected by a goddess. The four goddesses were Isis, her sister Nephthys, and two others whose names were Selket and Neith.

What other parts of the body did the Egyptians eventually remove in making a mummy? Strangely, they did not usually remove the kidneys. And they removed the heart only some of the time. The Egyptians believed that the heart was the center of intelligence, thought, and memory. So, of course, it was a very important organ.

In some New Kingdom burials, the heart was taken out of the body and mummified, and a carved stone in the shape of a beetle was put in its place. This beetle, of a type called a scarab, was common in Egypt from earliest times. It laid its eggs in a ball of dung, or manure, which it then rolled underground. The young scarabs hatched and fed on the dung. The Egyptians felt that new life rising from a ball of dung was a miracle. So the scarab became a symbol of immortality for them.

The wavy ridges at the top of the insect's head were believed to represent the rays of the sun. And the ball of dung became a symbol of the sun disk itself. Scarab designs appear over and over again in ancient Egyptian jewelry and in coffin and tomb decoration. The scarab design is still popular in jewelry today.

At other times in Egyptian history, the heart was dried and either put back in the body or placed elsewhere in the coffin with the mummy. Making mummies in ancient Egypt went on for about three thousand years. So even though the Egyptians were a people who kept to

The scarab with the sun disk, as it is often used in Egyptian jewelry designs

their traditions, ways of doing things were bound to change a little over so many centuries.

During the Old Kingdom and the Middle Kingdom, the Egyptians very seldom removed the brain in order to make a mummy. The brain simply remained in the skull and dried out naturally after a time. Some early mummies of this type were found in the last century. It was said that hardened bits of brain could actually be heard rattling around in the heads of these mummies when they were moved or shaken.

Starting with the New Kingdom, however, the Egyptians must have decided that it was important to remove the brain. The mummy of Ahmose, the first king of the Eighteenth Dynasty, shows that an incision was made in the back of his neck for this purpose. But soon the Egyptians found another way of extracting the brain. Although the new method was probably easier, most of us today find it shocking, even horrifying.

Placing a sharp instrument in the nostril, the mummy-makers broke through the bone between the top of the nasal cavity and the upper part of the skull. Then they inserted a long rod with a hook at the end through the nostril to the brain. The brain was either picked out piece by piece, or it was stirred until it became almost liquid. If the body was turned facedown, the contents of the brain would run out through the nostrils. Sometimes, water was poured into the brain cavity to help "rinse" it more completely.

The Egyptians never attempted to mummify the brain. One reason may be that they had no idea of its many important functions as a master organ of the body. Another may be that it was just too difficult to remove the brain in one piece without damaging the appearance of the mummy's head.

The next step in mummification was the drying out of the body itself. This was done by thickly coating it inside and out with a powdery white salt. This salt, known as natron, had the ability to draw water from the skin and other tissues.

The Egyptian desert was a plentiful source of natron. One famous gathering place was the oasis region of Wadi Natrun, about forty miles west of where Cairo, modern Egypt's capital city, lies. At this and other oases, underground water bubbled to the surface. The water contained the various salts, including ordinary table salt, of which natron is made up. As the surface water evaporated in the hot desert sun, clumps of this whitish substance appeared on the ground ready for use in mummification.

Drying the body in natron took from thirty-five to forty days. During that time, the corpse lay on a slanted board known as the "bed of mummification." The moisture dripped through a channel at the lower end into a pan or bucket. The body shrank as it lost its water content, and the skin became withered and leathery.

The odor of a slowly drying body, especially in the hot climate of Egypt, was very unpleasant. So both before and after the natron treatment, the body was cleansed inside and out with spices, sweet-smelling gums, and palm wine. The undertakers, or embalmers — those who prepared the bodies of the dead — were members of a trade that was handed down from father to son. Their work was respected and well paid. Yet they were disliked because of the smell of death that clung to them. It was

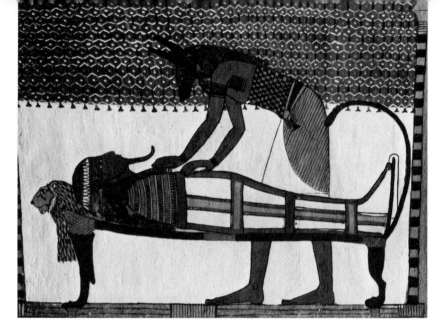

Tomb painting of a mummy lying on a slanted couch being attended to by the god Anubis

even the custom for the chief embalmer's assistants to go through a mock ceremony of throwing stones at him after he had opened the body and taken out the inner organs.

The organs themselves — those that had been removed to be placed in canopic jars — were dried in natron and treated the same way as the body. Because they were much smaller, they took less time to prepare.

Once the body was thoroughly dried, the abdominal cavity was packed with more natron and with fresh spices wrapped in linen. The cut that had been made in the left side of the abdomen to remove the organs was sewn up or sealed with resin. The nostrils might be plugged with wax and the mouth packed with pads of linen soaked in resin. The entire body was then rubbed with oil and "painted" with melted resin to give it a waterproof finish.

Now at last the time had come for wrapping and bandaging the mummy. A combination of large pieces of cloth and narrower strips of linen was used. The wrappings were applied in many layers. The mummy of a very important noble or a great king might have anywhere from sixteen or twenty layers of wrapping to as many as eighty. The layers added up to a thickness of one-half inch to about two inches, and the entire wrapping process is believed to have taken fifteen days or more.

The wrappings covered whatever jewelry — necklaces, collars, girdles, bracelets, anklets, and rings — had been placed on the mummy. Precious objects were also tucked in between the layers of bandages. Many were charms to ensure the mummy's afterlife, such as the eye of Horus, the scarab, and the ankh. The ankh, a cross with a looped top, was the Egyptian sign for life. In many New Kingdom burials, each finger and toe of the mummy was encased in a thimble-like sheath, or tube, of solid gold.

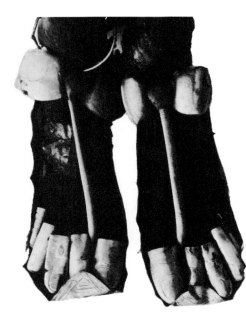

The feet of the mummy of King Tutankhamen wearing gold sandals with turned-up points, and with each toe encased in a solid-gold tube

The name of the dead person was marked on the ends of the linen bandages. Many centuries later, royal mummies that had been stripped of their jewelry and nearly destroyed by tomb robbers were identified by the shreds of bandages still clinging to their bodies.

As the layers of bandages were applied, warm melted resin was poured over each one, again for the purpose of keeping moisture from entering the body. Unfortunately, the resin tended to darken the skin. In the case of the famous king Tutankhamen (Toot-ahnk-AH-men), too many body oils and resins were used. The two substances interacted chemically after the tomb was sealed, forming a sticky, gummy, black mass. When the king's burial chamber was discovered, over three thousand years after his death, his mummy was found to be stuck fast to the bottom of the coffin in which it lay. Only tatters of leathery flesh still clung to the bones.

Most of the mummies of Tutankhamen's time, however, were very well preserved, right down to the details of their hair and eyelashes. Even so, the Egyptians strove to make still better mummies, ones that were less wrinkled and shrunken.

By the Twenty-first Dynasty, they had begun to give their mummies the equivalent of the modern face-lift. They made artful slits in the face, neck, arms, and legs of the mummy and inserted filling materials between the skin and the muscle layer beneath it. Sawdust, ashes, mud, sand, and linen packing were used to give a plump, rounded, lifelike appearance to the face and body. Now, too, artificial eyes of stone or painted linen were added along with false eyebrows made of human hair.

The blackened and poorly preserved mummy of King Tutankhamen

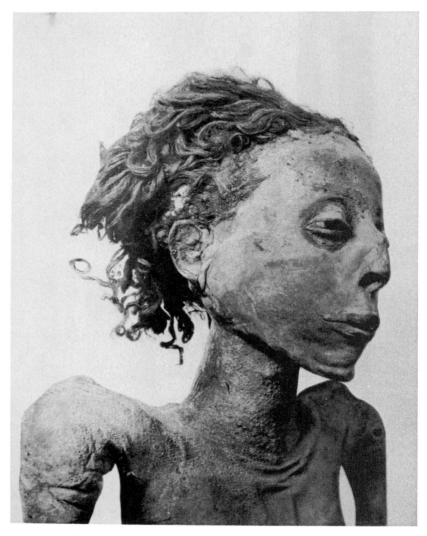

Mummy of a priestess of the 22nd Dynasty with face and shoulders packed with sawdust, eyes of painted stone, and false human hair

To make the bodies more complete, the mummified organs were put back in their proper places in the abdominal cavity. But the Egyptians continued to observe tradition by keeping a set of empty canopic jars protected by the four sons of Horus in the tomb as well.

From the Twenty-fifth Dynasty onward, the appearance of the mummy itself became less important than the wrapping. Also, the organs were once again stored in canopic jars or wrapped in linen and placed in the coffin between the legs of the mummy. Perhaps the Egyptians now considered it too much bother to put them back in the body.

Much of what we know about how mummies were made comes to us from the famous Greek historian Herodotus (Heh-ROD-uh-tus). He visited Egypt in the 400s B.C. during the rule of the Twenty-seventh Dynasty, and wrote a careful description of the methods that were used. At that time, and for centuries past, a proper royal mummification had taken seventy days.

Soon after the reporting of Herodotus, though, the Egyptians began speeding up the process of mummification. They shortened or omitted the natron treatment in many cases, and instead coated the bodies inside and out with a thick, black, tarry substance called pitch. The mummies were heavy and solid. Although they were fairly well preserved, they were also brittle and broke easily.

Later, when the Greeks and then the Romans ruled Egypt, the mummy's wrappings became the most elaborate they had ever been. The outer layers were arranged in intricate diamond shapes or other geometric patterns.

Sometimes they were decorated with golden studs. Heads were covered with painted portrait masks that resembled the dead as they had appeared in life.

Who *were* all the Egyptians who were mummified from the time of Queen Hetepheres way back in the Fourth Dynasty? When artificial mummification first began in Egypt, it was intended only for kings and their immediate families. But as early as the Fifth Dynasty, nobles, priests, government officials, and wealthy land-owners also began to be mummified. They, too, were buried in handsome tombs that were provided with all the necessities and luxuries for the afterlife. Less wealthy people had shorter periods of mummification and more modest burials. It was all a question of what one could afford.

The very poorest Egyptians were either partially preserved and buried in a common pit with a few belongings or simply wrapped in a coarse cloth and put in a hole in the sand, as in the very early days when only natural mummification was known. Interestingly, their bodies often outlasted those of the rich and powerful. No tomb robbers came to plunder their graves. And the hot desert sands could still be relied upon to make better mummies than some of the overly ambitious royal undertakers.

The Egyptians, however, had become so involved in making mummies that, starting at about the time of the New Kingdom, they actually began to mummify animals.

This strange practice came about because nearly every Egyptian god and goddess was linked to a particular animal. Even gods who were usually shown as having

The god Amen-Ra, usually pictured in human form, shown with the head of a ram and the body of a lion at the entrance to the Temple of Karnak

human heads and bodies were identified with animals that were sacred to them. In turn, these animals became sacred to the Egyptian people.

Live animals were kept at the temples that were dedicated to the various gods. When the animals died, they were mummified and buried at the temple itself or in special tombs.

As time went on, some animals were killed on purpose, and greater and greater numbers were sacrificed in this way. They included falcons sacred to the sun god, Ra; baboons and ibises sacred to Thoth, the god of writing; dogs and jackals sacred to Anubis; cats sacred to the goddess Bast; and also fish, crocodiles, rodents, snakes, and even insects.

Larger animals, too, were mummified, but in fewer

43

Mummified cats, sacred to Bast, the goddess of pleasure

numbers. The largest was the so-called Apis, or sacred bull. He represented the god Osiris and was also considered the son of Isis, who was often shown wearing the horns of a cow as a headdress.

Only one bull, specially selected at birth, was kept at the Apis temple at a time. When he died, his body was treated much like that of one of Egypt's kings. His internal organs, however, were not removed. Instead, his body was pumped with strong fluids. Then it was thoroughly dried. The entire process, as for a human, took seventy days. After a while, even the cows who were the mothers of the Apis bulls were mummified!

In recent times, experiments have been done on chickens and other animals to see if mummification as practiced by the ancient Egyptians really works. And it does! An even more telling experiment was carried out on a human corpse by a German doctor. He "pulped" the brain to a liquid exactly as was done by the mummifiers of the New Kingdom and found that it could indeed be made to run out through the nostrils. So the age-old mysteries of how to make a mummy turned out to be not so secret after all.

The next step, of course, for the mummies of ancient Egypt was the journey to the tomb, or the "house of eternity," as it was known. What were the "houses of eternity" that the wealthy and powerful Egyptians chose for themselves? And how did the simple, stone grave markers of the early Nile dwellers grow into massive, towering pyramids and intricate cliffside tombs cut out of solid rock?

A mastaba built of mud bricks. A side view shows two chapels, deep filled-in shaft, and burial chamber.

4

The Mummy's Tomb

Up to about the time that Upper and Lower Egypt were united into one kingdom, the Nile farmers had been building their houses out of coarsely packed mud and reeds. Quite soon afterward, however, they began using sun-dried bricks instead. As the dwellings of the living improved, so did the "houses of eternity" in which the dead would "live." A heap of stones or a large rock was no longer a suitable grave marker for an important person. Therefore, starting with the First Dynasty, it became the custom for the kings of Egypt to be buried beneath a structure known as a mastaba (MAHS-tah-bah).

A mastaba was a rectangular mud-brick tomb with a flat roof and sloping sides. In many ways it resembled a village house. It also followed the shape of the sort of bench that was often found in front of such a house, and is even seen in Egypt today. The very word *mastaba* is Arabic for "bench."

Some of the mastabas of the First and Second Dynasty rulers were very grand. They were much larger than ordinary houses and had rooms both aboveground and below. There was usually a chapel aboveground in which offerings of food could be made to the dead.

But the actual burial place of the king was some forty to eighty feet underground, at the bottom of a deep, narrow shaft. There lay his bejeweled mummy in its coffin, along with his treasured possessions for the afterlife. Often, too, there was an image of the king in the mummy chamber. It was carved out of wood or stone. In case anything happened to the mummy, it was hoped that the king's statue would serve as a substitute so that his *ka* and his *ba* would not die.

After everything had been carefully placed in the burial chamber, the shaft was filled with closely packed broken stones. Then it was sealed up and the entrance to it from inside the mastaba was cleverly concealed. Even so, tomb robbers almost always managed to find the underground chamber and carry off its buried treasure. Often they did this by tunneling a long, sloping ramp down through the sand, starting their digging some distance away from the mastaba itself.

By the Third Dynasty, the kings of Egypt were becoming very powerful. The squat, flat-topped mastaba no longer seemed like a fitting "house of eternity." So Imhotep, the vizier, or prime minister, of an important king called Zoser, tried something new. He expanded the mastaba into a very large, square building. Then he placed five more square mastabas, each one smaller than the others, on top of it.

Imhotep, who was a mathematician, engineer, and ar-

The step pyramid of King Zoser

chitect, and was also said to be learned in medicine, had created what was known as the step pyramid. Unlike the mud-brick mastabas, it was made entirely of stone and it soared to a height of two hundred feet, or about twenty stories.

The inside of the pyramid was nearly all solid stone. Like the mastabas, though, it had a deep burial chamber that lay almost one hundred feet underground. The chamber was part of a maze of secret rooms, some of them lined with beautiful blue tiles. But it too was discovered by ancient robbers who probably stripped the mummy. Only a foot and some other parts of the body believed to be that of King Zoser have ever been found.

The step pyramid of King Zoser, at Sakkara in northern Egypt, still stands today. Even though part of the bottom layer has crumbled, its six stages can be made out clearly. The only structure of its kind, it is an amazing link between the early mastabas and the huge slope-sided pyramids that were to follow.

Many people have wondered why the Egyptians chose the pyramid as a tomb for the most powerful rulers of the Old Kingdom. The word *pyramid* is from the Greek. In fact, these pointed stone structures may have been named for the cone-shaped loaves of wheat bread that were eaten in ancient Greece.

The ancient Egyptian word for pyramid, however, is *mer*, meaning "place of ascent." It seems right, then, to guess that the Egyptians thought of the pyramid as a "stairway to the heavens." This seems even truer when we learn that the entrances to the pyramids of the Old Kingdom were always on the north side. The Egyptians believed that the king's soul would find its way out the door and upward to the northern polar stars, which, in Egypt, are never seen to set. Thus, the king would dwell forever among the undying stars.

At the same time, a pyramid seen from the top down resembles the outward-slanting rays of the sun. Starting in the Old Kingdom, the Egyptians built four-sided columns called obelisks to the sun god, Ra. They topped the columns with cones that looked like miniature pyramids and covered the cones with gold or other shiny metals that would glitter in Ra's brilliant light. So the purpose of the pyramid-shaped tomb may also have been to direct the king's soul heavenward to join the sun god.

The kings of the Fourth Dynasty were the great pyramid builders of all time. One early king named Sneferu (Sneh-FAY-roo) got off to a rather shaky start with the so-called "bent" pyramid. This odd structure has smooth sides but changes its angle of slope about halfway to the top. Perhaps it had to be finished in a hurry, or the workers ran short of building materials. Still it does reach a

A fallen obelisk and two standing ones with pyramid-shaped tops that were once capped with gold

height of well over three hundred feet. And it has a beautiful outer coating of fine white limestone.

The most famous Egyptian pyramids are the three that were built on the flat desert sands at Giza. This site, on the western bank of the Nile, was close to the Old Kingdom capital of Memphis in Lower Egypt.

The largest, or Great Pyramid, was constructed for King Khufu. It was four hundred eighty feet, or nearly fifty stories, high. Over two million blocks of stone averaging two-and-a-half tons, with some weighing as much as fifteen tons, were used. One hundred thousand men were said to have labored on the Great Pyramid for twenty years.

The second and third Giza pyramids were somewhat smaller and were built for King Khufu's successors, Khafre (KAH-fray) and Menkaure (Men-KAW-ray). The pyramid of Menkaure is the smallest of the three. Surprisingly, Khafre's pyramid appears taller than that of Khufu. But that is because it was built on higher ground.

Also, Khufu's pyramid has lost all of its outer facing of smooth white limestone blocks, making it many feet shorter than it was originally. Khafre's pyramid still has a capping of limestone. The practice of stripping the limestone finishes from the pyramids took place in later times. It was ordered by rulers who wanted this handsome building material for their own palaces and places of worship.

Almost directly in front of the pyramid of Khafre sits the mysterious figure of the Great Sphinx. This mythical creature with a human head and the body of a lion is carved out of desert rock. No one is certain, but many people believe that the face is meant to be that of King Khafre.

The pyramid of King Khafre with the Great Sphinx in the foreground

In most of the Old Kingdom pyramids, the king's burial chamber was hidden underground. It was reached by a downward-sloping shaft that began somewhere on the north side of the pyramid. The Great Pyramid, though, is an exception. There the king's chamber was found *inside* the pyramid, about halfway to the top. The pyramid also has an unfinished underground shaft and a smaller chamber beneath the king's chamber that is wrongly called the queen's chamber. Both of these are thought to have been earlier choices for burial that were abandoned because the higher chamber seemed safer. But no place was really safe. For Khufu's tomb, sealed into the stone heart of his Great Pyramid, was discovered and robbed like all the others.

In death, the kings held court just as they had in life. Their tall pyramids did not stand alone in the desert. They were surrounded by an assortment of lesser buildings, including small pyramids, mastabas, and temples. Queens and other members of the royal family, prime ministers and other officials, priests, and lesser nobles were all buried in these nearby tombs. Often there were "streets" of mastabas laid out around the king's pyramid. The mastaba, now built of stone rather than mud brick, continued to be used as a burial structure for wealthy Egyptians. Later even rich commoners adopted the mastaba.

The pyramid temples were of two kinds. Closest to the riverbank was the so-called valley temple. It was here that the king's body was brought by barge to undergo mummification. A long walkway led across the desert sands to the offering temple, which was set in

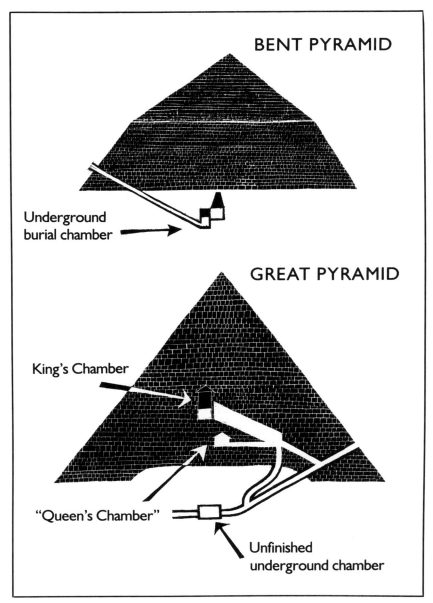

BENT PYRAMID

Underground
burial chamber

GREAT PYRAMID

King's Chamber

"Queen's Chamber"

Unfinished
underground chamber

*The Bent Pyramid and the Great Pyramid, showing location of
burial chambers*

front of the pyramid. In this temple, ceremonies were held honoring the dead king.

Pyramids and other tombs were built on the west bank of the Nile, just beyond the fertile strip of black land, where the desert or red land began. The Egyptians chose the west bank as the "land of the dead" because that was where the dying sun disappeared each evening.

The building of the pyramids was generally started during the dry season of May and June. That was when the Nile River was at its lowest level. The crops of the year before had been harvested, and the ground was now dry and cracked under a baking sun. The farmers had no field work to do until after the Nile had once again risen and flooded its banks, starting in July and lasting through September.

The farmers turned pyramid-builders were paid for their labor in food and clothing, and were provided with tools. There were no coins or other types of money used in Egypt at that time. Many of the farmers probably worked on the pyramids of their own free will rather than as forced labor. The work was a means of adding to their livelihood.

Once the Nile flood began, barges were able to bring stones downriver from the more distant quarries and to unload them quite close to the building sites at the desert's edge. The river was Egypt's main highway, used to transport all sorts of goods.

But most of the stone used in the pyramids came from the surrounding desert itself. On land, the stones were transported on sleds with wide wooden runners. Wheels would probably have been useless; they would have sunk at once into the sand.

A 4000-year-old model of one of the many kinds of wooden rowing boats used on the Nile. The model was found in a Middle Kingdom tomb.

Astonishingly, every step of the work was accomplished with human labor. The enormous blocks of stone were cut and shaped by hand with tools of flint or copper, because the Egyptians had no iron. The stones were lifted and hauled onto the sleds with the help of wooden wedges and stout wooden bars used as levers. The sleds themselves were pulled not by animals but by teams of men. The oxen and donkeys that the Egyptians used for field work could not have been watered and fed in the harsh desert.

As the pyramid grew taller, the blocks of stone roped to their sleds were pulled uphill on ramps made of rocks, sand, and mud. Logs, laid crosswise on the ramps, were embedded in the mud every few feet. They acted as stoppers to keep the heavy sleds from rolling backward.

Any interior rooms or passages had to be finished off before the upper part of the pyramid was completed. In Khufu's Great Pyramid, the king's huge stone coffin was lowered into place in the burial chamber when the pyramid was only about half-built. After the king died, his body was brought to the chamber in a smaller wooden coffin through an inside passageway.

In the final centuries of the Old Kingdom and also during the Middle Kingdom, pyramids continued to be built in Egypt. After the Fourth Dynasty, though, there were none to rival those at Giza. Some Fifth Dynasty pyramids were so poorly constructed atop their underground burial chambers that they collapsed over the years into mounds of broken stones and gravel. The builders of the Middle Kingdom pyramids did learn one thing from the Old Kingdom builders. They no longer placed the entrance to the pyramid on the north side, for this was a sure giveaway to thieves as to the route to the burial chamber.

Altogether there were about eighty pyramids built for the kings of Egypt. But not one proved a safe and secure burial place. The pyramid itself drew attention to the great wealth within it or just beneath it. And so, sooner or later, all were robbed of their treasure.

By the time of the New Kingdom, a number of changes had taken place in Egypt. For one thing, the capital no longer lay in the northern part of the country. It had been moved south to a place in Upper Egypt called Thebes.

The kings were now wealthier and stronger than ever. They had large armies equipped with bronze spears and daggers as well as earlier battle weapons like clubs, axes,

Prisoners of war from Nubia bowing to their Egyptian captors

slingshots, and bows and arrows. They even had chariots and horses. These two had been introduced to Egypt by an Asiatic people called the Hyksos who had invaded and temporarily ruled Egypt during the Second Intermediate Period. Before that time, horses and wheeled vehicles were practically unknown in Egypt.

The troops themselves included Asiatics; Libyans, who came from the western borders of Egypt; and Nubians, who came from the far south. Some were slaves, originally taken as prisoners. But many were mercenaries, or paid foreign soldiers, for the Egyptians themselves seemed to prefer farming or other stay-at-home occupations to army life.

Egypt now ruled lands beyond its borders, in Asia and in Africa, and the king had come to be called a pharaoh (FAY-roh), which means "great house." To speak of the pharaoh was like saying "the palace," when one really meant the ruler who lived there. It was a sign of deep respect shown to the powerful royalty of the New Kingdom.

At Thebes, the landscape was somewhat different from that in the north. The Nile was narrower and the river's west bank was walled with harsh, forbidding desert cliffs. If this rugged land of the setting sun was to be the "city of the dead" for the New Kingdom rulers, the building of great, broad-based pyramids was out of the question. Anyhow, by this time everybody knew that pyramids didn't work and weren't a good idea.

So a new burial structure known as the rock-cut tomb began to be built. Burial caverns tunneled into natural rock had been constructed in earlier times in hilly places in Egypt. But none were as large or as intricate as those of some of the New Kingdom pharaohs. The tomb of King Seti I, with its corridors, staircases, and series of elegant underground rooms, was over three hundred feet long.

The tombs also contained false doors, tunnels that changed direction, and blocked passages to deceive and confuse thieves. And their outside entrances were concealed in the rock faces of the cliffs and fortified with sealed, rock-filled entry shafts.

There were some temples built on the west bank at Thebes, like that of Queen Hatshepsut (Hat-SHEP-sut), the only female pharaoh of the New Kingdom. But such temples were no longer placed anywhere near the secret burial sites of the same rulers in order to avoid attracting tomb robbers.

The temple of Queen Hatshepsut set against the desert cliff on the west bank of the Nile

Even so, of about sixty rock-cut tombs discovered in the Valley of the Kings at Thebes, all but that of King Tutankhamen were thoroughly ransacked in ancient times. The same was true of the nearby Valley of the Queens, which contained the tombs of not only queens but also princes and other nobles.

If the Egyptians knew that these burial places were going to be robbed, why did they go on burying their mummies with so many body jewels and valuable tomb furnishings?

One answer may have been that the Egyptians were deeply bound to tradition. They were devoted to their beliefs and slow to change their ways. Probably another reason was their faith in the magical power of images.

The coffin might be broken into and hacked to pieces. Rings, bracelets, anklets, and other charms might be stolen. The mummy itself might be destroyed and with it the statuary that had been placed in the chamber. But there was one thing the thieves could not take away with them — the pictures that had been painted or carved on the tomb walls.

Those pictures not only preserved the dead in scenes from life — at games and pastimes, at banquets, at outdoor sports, and overseeing the everyday activities on their estates. They also showed the dead with Osiris and other gods going through the stages of entry into the afterlife.

For nothing was more important to the Egyptians than the life to come after death. And the tomb itself was really just the starting point for the journey of the soul toward eternity, the world of forever.

The walls of this rock-cut tomb are covered with scenes of both life on earth and the passage into the afterlife.

Hunting waterfowl in the Nile marshes. This pastime of wealthy Egyptians was thought to continue in the afterlife.

5
The Mummy's Afterlife

The funeral processions of ancient Egypt must have attracted large crowds of curious onlookers. In Thebes, during the New Kingdom, the preparations were especially dramatic.

Most people lived on the east bank of the Nile. But as soon as death struck, the body of the deceased was transported by boat to the "city of the dead" on the grim, stony west bank to be mummified. While the dead person was being prepared for the afterlife, the family went into a period of deep mourning. Men didn't shave, women wore torn garments and neglected their appearance, and everyone ate sparingly during the seventy days of mummification.

At last the day of burial arrived, and a great procession was formed starting out from the house of the dead person. It featured an empty, newly made coffin on a wooden sled pulled by oxen. The coffin would be taken across the river by boat to the place of mummification to fetch the mummy and transport it to its tomb.

Mourners and servants followed the coffin on foot. The servants of the wealthy were strung out in long lines, carrying articles of furniture and numerous chests containing clothing, toilet articles, cosmetics, oils and perfumes, wigs, and other personal belongings.

To pass the time in the afterlife, as in the life that had gone before, the dead were also provided with game boards, bows and arrows, throwing sticks, and other types of hunting gear. The long procession, with its burdened servants, must have made one think of moving day.

Because the servants would be accompanying their dead master or mistress only as far as the tomb, the mummy chamber would also be supplied with miniature figures of servants known as *shabti*s, or "answerers." The doll-like *shabti*s were usually made of wood, stone, or pottery. They ranged in size from a few inches to over a foot tall. Their purpose was not merely to wait on the dead. They were intended to act as stand-ins for the dead should Osiris ask the mummy to perform duties like field work or irrigation on his estates in the land of the hereafter.

*Shabti*s were first found in tombs of the Middle Kingdom. But usually there was only one to a tomb. In the New Kingdom tombs, even some of the lesser nobles had as many as four hundred and one *shabti*s. This figure was arrived at by adding three hundred and sixty-five, or one for each day of the year, plus thirty-six "overseers," or one for each week of the year. The Egyptians, at that time, had a ten-day week, so there were thirty-six full weeks in a year.

Wooden shabtis *found in the tomb of King Ramses VI*

Royal tombs had even more *shabti*s. Over seven hundred were found in the tomb of King Seti I. The *shabti*s were not often stolen by grave robbers unless they were made of gold or of wood covered with a coating of gold leaf.

Like the servants, the mourners walked in the funeral procession, following directly behind the coffin on its sled. At the river's edge, the procession temporarily broke ranks for the short crossing to the opposite shore. The waiting boats were made of bunched papyrus reeds. Among the items loaded onto them was a second smaller sled. It would bear to the tomb the boxlike chest containing the canopic jars in which lay the mummified organs of the deceased.

Once the opposite shore had been reached and the mummy laid in its coffin, the procession reformed itself. Now it began to wind its way up into the foothills of the harsh desert cliffs. The mourning women showed their grief with loud wailing. They tore their garments and

A group of mourning women, some pouring dust on their heads to show grief

The Opening of the Mouth ceremony

covered their heads with dust scooped up from the ground. Often there were hired mourners as well. Their shrieks and moans added to the din, as if intended to reach the ears of the mummy itself.

Upon arrival at the tomb site, the footsore procession was more than ready to rest and be refreshed with a funerary banquet. The freshly cooked food for the meal had also been brought along by the family servants of the dead person.

An unusual guest at the banquet was the mummy itself. Before the meal began, a ceremony known as the Opening of the Mouth took place. The bandaged mummy, often strapped to a board, was made to stand upright in its coffin or might be taken out of the coffin. It was supported by a priest wearing a mask representing the jackal-headed god, Anubis. Meantime, two other priests touched the mouth, eyes, and ears of the mummy with a wand-like instrument, while a high priest dressed in a traditional leopard skin looked on.

This act was said to give the mummy the ability to eat, speak, see, hear, and move about in the afterlife. Now the dead person was believed to be able to share in the funeral meal. The mummy had also been given the magical power to eat the food that would be left in the tomb, as well as the food that would later be brought to the offering temple. Of course, as the Egyptians interpreted it, it was the dead person's *ka*, or soul, that would "eat" in the afterlife rather than the mummy itself.

The funeral-banquet foods were the same as those found on the tables of the wealthier classes throughout Egypt. The meal might include roast ox, sheep, or goat, ducks and geese, and perhaps some wild game or waterfowl. The Egyptians had no chickens or turkeys. Pigs were raised, but they seem to have been considered unclean. Their meat may have been eaten only by the poor. Fish, too, usually did not appear at funeral banquets, even though the Nile was a plentiful source. Some varieties were considered sacred and were forbidden as food. Perhaps another reason was that fish did not keep well in Egypt's hot climate.

The guests at the funeral meal drank wine and the juices of dates and pomegranates. Beer, which was made from fermented wheat and barley, was the drink of most Egyptians. Unlike the meat-rich diet of the wealthy, the poor lived mainly on bread, onions, and dried beans and lentils. Along with beer, those were the foods that were supplied to the workers who built the pyramids, temples, and other great monuments of ancient Egypt.

Once the funeral banquet was over, the mummy with all its belongings and provisions of food was sealed into

Servants harvesting grapes for wine on the estate of an Egyptian noble

its tomb, and the mourners returned home. Often they left behind the wreathlike collars of flowers and leaves that they wore at the banquet. Such collars, withered and dried, have been found around the necks of the mummies as well.

The families of the dead were only partly consoled by the mummy's presence at the funeral meal. To assure themselves that the *ka* would continue to be fed, they might bring food and drink to the offering temple regularly. Or they might pay the priests to do so. In the New Kingdom, the offering temples were always built at some distance from the tomb itself to keep thieves away from the mummy and its buried treasure.

Who ate the food that was left at the offering temple? Perhaps it was the priests themselves. Or maybe the food was given to the poor. In any case, the offerings were bound to stop after a time, as the families died off and the priests were no longer paid for this service. The Egyptians believed that then the paintings on the tomb walls, showing servants bringing food, would alone sustain the *ka* through eternity.

A successful life in the hereafter, however, depended on more than food alone. To ensure that the dead person would "live again," there were many tests and trials to overcome. So coffins, tomb walls, and scrolls of papyrus that were buried with the mummy were covered with magic writings, spells, and charms. The Egyptians believed the writings had the power to lead the dead safely past demons and monsters into the presence of the gods. Such writings are known as Pyramid Texts, Coffin Texts, or, if they were inscribed on papyrus, as Books of the Dead.

Papyrus was the Egyptian "paper." One could write on it in ink with a reed brush. The paperlike sheets were made by pressing together thin, water-soaked strips cut from the tall stalks of the papyrus plant, which grew in the Nile marshes. Sheets of papyrus were costly, however, so most Egyptian writing was carved into stone or wood.

The picture writing of the Egyptians, called hieroglyphics (high-er-oh-GLIF-iks), or "sacred carvings," probably came into existence some time before Upper and Lower Egypt were united into one kingdom. But only a small proportion of Egyptians ever learned how to read and write.

Hieroglyphic writing inside oval-shaped scrolls, as depicted in stone carvings

Among them were the scribes, or official writers, who were specially educated for this job. Many scribes served as public letter-writers, clerks, tax-collectors, or record-keepers in the granaries and warehouses. Even a child from a poor peasant family could greatly improve his life by mastering the art of writing. There were scribes who rose to positions of wealth and importance as government administrators, diplomats, and advisers to royalty.

Sometime after the last dynasty died out, however, the reading and writing of hieroglyphics began to be forgotten. For well over the next thousand years, nobody knew the meaning of the mysterious markings that covered the temples, tombs, and other ancient monuments of Egypt.

Today we are able to read the picture writing of the Egyptians because of the discovery of the Rosetta Stone. This four-foot-high black stone covered with strange lettering, was found in 1799 by an officer of the army of the famous French general Napoleon. The French were occupying Egypt at that time.

Half-buried in the mud near a northerly branch of the Nile, the stone took its name from the not-far-distant town of Rosetta. It turned out to be inscribed with lettering in three different languages. Two were forms of Egyptian hieroglyphics and the third was Greek. A French language specialist named Jean François Champollion translated the Greek. Then, guessing that the message in all three languages was the same, he found clues that gradually helped him to "break the code" of the Egyptian symbols. In 1822, Champollion succeeded in making out the full meaning of the two sets of hieroglyphic writing.

The message on the Rosetta Stone had been inscribed in 196 B.C. It honored a Greek ruler Ptolemy V, who was then king of Egypt. But more important, it opened the way for us to read once again the ancient Egyptian language. This knowledge has greatly increased our understanding of how the Egyptians both lived and died.

From the time of the New Kingdom, it was the custom for even quite poor Egyptian families to place a Book of the Dead in the coffin or wrappings of the mummy. Ready-made papyrus scrolls, containing up to two hundred magic spells, could be bought from the scribes. There was a spell to keep the body from rotting, a spell to help the mummy reach the next world safely, a spell

The prosperous overseer of the scribes of an Old Kingdom granary with his wife and son. The boy wears his hair braided to one side in a style known as the "sidelock of youth."

to prevent one from dying a second death in the afterlife, and so on. All the family had to do was to choose a scroll it could afford and fill in the name of the dead person in the spaces that had been left blank.

Wealthier Egyptians had their Books of the Dead written especially for them by certain well-paid scribes. No two were alike. And the scribes themselves often prepared beautifully illustrated scrolls to be placed in their own tombs.

In the Book of the Dead of the scribe Ani, one of the important ceremonies for entry into the afterlife is pictured in detail. This was the ceremony of the Weighing of the Heart ordered by Maat, the Egyptian goddess of truth and justice.

The scene shows a balance scale on which Ani's heart is being weighed against a feather, the symbol of Maat. The god Anubis adjusts the scale. To his right, Thoth, the ibis-headed god of writing, stands ready to record the result of the trial. A baboon, sacred to Thoth, perches atop the center support of the scale.

If Ani's heart is heavier than the feather, he will not be allowed to enter the afterlife. In fact, he will be destroyed by a hideous monster — Ammit, the Devourer. This "eater of the dead" stands just behind Thoth, ready to pounce. It has the head of a crocodile, the forequarters of a lion, and the hindquarters of a hippopotamus.

To the left of the picture, Ani, accompanied by his wife, leans forward as he prays that his heart will be found to be so empty of evil that it will weigh less than the feather of Maat.

No one knows if a dead pharaoh, a noted scribe, or a

The Weighing of the Heart ceremony as illustrated in the Book of the Dead of the scribe Ani

prosperous landowner passed or failed this test. All Egyptians wanted to believe, *had* to believe, that those who had died had been granted a safe and successful passage to the afterlife. That was what they themselves hoped for when their time came for the Opening of the Mouth, the Weighing of the Heart, and the meeting at last with the great god Osiris.

A chestpiece of gold and semi-precious jewels found in the tomb of Tutankhamen with scarab and eye of Horus designs, falcon's wings, and cobras' heads

6

The Mummy's Treasure and the Tomb Robbers

Who were the tomb robbers who stole almost all of the buried treasure of ancient Egypt? How did *they* feel about the all-important afterlife? And weren't they frightened of the terrible punishments that were given to those who were caught plundering the sacred burial places?

The tomb robbers came from many walks of life. They ranged from lowly laborers to corrupt priests and government officials. They must have included artisans and artists, tomb architects and police guards. In other words, anybody who had anything to do with designing or building a tomb or preparing or burying a mummy had enough knowledge to rob a tomb or to sell maps and other information to those who were tomb robbers by profession.

Grave robbing even became a family business in Egypt. Its secrets were handed down from father to son. One village had an especially bad reputation as the home of a family of tomb robbers. Not surprisingly, it was located on the west bank of the Nile not far from the treasure-filled Valley of the Kings.

Some of the tomb robbers may indeed have believed in the afterlife. But they were more interested in ensuring their own life after death rather than that of their victims. With the riches they stole, they too could have a handsome tomb with painted walls and books of magic spells that would work miracles in the hereafter. Other tomb robbers probably cared more about a prosperous life on earth than about any that was promised after death.

Gold was always in great demand in Egypt. Some of it was mined in the desert that lay in the eastern half of the country. But much of it came from the region far to the south called Nubia. This was the land of the Nile rapids and gushing waterfalls that were known as cataracts.

A village, similar to those of the tomb-robbing families, built on the stony heights near the Valley of the Kings

To hide the source of their booty, the robbers melted down the gold jewelry and other objects containing gold that they stole. Wooden articles that were covered with a thin crust of gold were burned to melt off the metal. The beautiful workmanship that added so much to the value of the grave goods was lost forever.

The Egyptians had no precious stones such as diamonds, rubies, or sapphires. But semi-precious gems like turquoise, garnet, carnelian, lapis lazuli, and amethyst were worked into jewelry, often in settings of gold. Ivory, imported from Nubia and other lands to the south, was also in demand by thieves. And often the robbers stole the oils and unguents, or salves, that had been deposited in the tombs.

Wealthy Egyptians protected their bodies against the drying effects of the sun with these valuable substances. They were costly because the trees and plants from which they came were rare in Egypt. The plants grew mainly in western Asia, so the precious oils had to be imported.

The perfumes and cosmetics of the wealthy were sought after, too. Women and sometimes men wore cones of wax containing perfume atop their heads. As the wax slowly melted in the heat, the face, head, and shoulders became pleasantly scented.

The cosmetics in the tombs included gray-black or dark-green pastes that were made from ground-up minerals and were known as kohl. In life, women used these pastes to darken their eyelids and outline their eyes. Men, too, rimmed and extended their eyes with kohl. Women reddened their lips and cheeks with another mineral pigment called ocher. Henna, a red-orange plant

A wealthy Egyptian and his wife, wearing wax perfume cones and finely pleated linen garments, worshipping the gods of the dead

dye, was used to tint the nails, the palms of the hands, and the soles of the feet. Luckily for us, the tomb robbers left behind many of the articles from the makeup chests placed in the tombs of the ladies of ancient Egypt. Among them were tiny spoons and brushes, small glass and alabaster pots and jars, and polished bronze hand mirrors.

Unfortunately the robbers were often very cruel to the mummies themselves. Working hastily, they did not hesitate to smash the stone coffin lids and slash at the mummy's bandages to get at the jewelry inside the wrappings. Arms or legs might be pulled off the bodies, and in some cases, the stripped mummies were actually burned to provide light by which to loot the rest of the tomb. The brittle bodies, coated with hardened resin, gave a bright flame.

The punishments dealt out to those caught at tomb robbing were truly terrible. The living criminal might have a stake driven through his body, his hands chopped off, or his nose and ears cut off. Or he might be taken out to the desert, bound hand and foot, and left there to die. Even so, the tomb robbing, which had begun on a major scale with the mastaba burials of the early kings, continued through the centuries.

In the closing years of the New Kingdom, around 1100 B.C., robberies increased dramatically. Most likely this was simply because it was an age of great wealth for Egypt and there were so many rich tombs to rob. But some historians think there was another reason as well.

In the part of Asia that was closest to Egypt, the Iron Age had arrived. People learned to mine and work iron into sturdy tools and weapons. Egypt, however, did not have large iron deposits. It was still making most of its tools out of bronze, a mixture of copper and tin. Egypt was forced to import iron. This caused such an increase in taxes and in the cost of living that many more people turned to thievery.

Whatever the reason, around 1000 B.C. a group of priests of the Twenty-first Dynasty took steps to rescue the tattered remains of some of the royal mummies whose graves had been looted. They found an abandoned tomb near the temple of Queen Hatshepsut and secretly transferred the mummies to the new hiding place. Many were re-bandaged and marked with their names taken from the old wrappings. Even the dates of rewrapping were inscribed on the cloth. Some of the mummies were given new coffins. Also reburied with them were those belongings the thieves had ignored as being of lesser value. Among them were papyrus scrolls, canopic jars, and *shabti*s.

For nearly three thousand years the mummies rested peacefully in their new home. Then, in 1875, unusual objects began to appear for sale in the shops, hotels, and bazaars of Luxor. This new city had sprung to life on the east bank of the Nile, on the site of ancient Thebes. Ever since the early 1800s, when Egypt's past had begun to be revealed through the discovery of the Rosetta Stone, the country had been swarming with foreign visitors. Among them were tourists, souvenir seekers, art collectors, and archeologists who were studying the monuments and digging for the remains of Egypt's ancient civilization.

The mysterious objects that were coming on the market turned out to be scrolls, *shabti*s, and other articles belonging to various rulers of the New Kingdom and of the Twenty-first Dynasty, which followed it. Finally, in 1881, the Egyptian government tracked down the source of the articles. Sure enough, one of the old tomb-robbing families had been at work again. A pair of brothers had discovered the hiding place of the mummies near the temple of Queen Hatshepsut.

Aside from the items they had stolen, the modern tomb robbers had done little further damage to the mummies. Among them were such famed rulers of the New Kingdom as Ahmose, Amenhotep I, Thutmose I, II, and II, Seti I, and Ramses I, II, and III. With great care, the mummies were transported to Cairo where many can be seen today in the Mummy Room of the Cairo Museum.

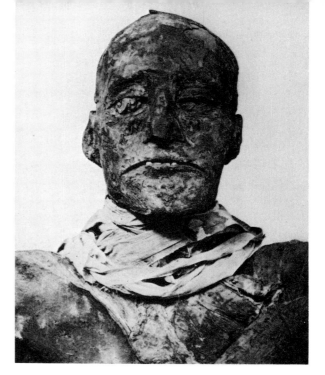

The mummy of Ramses III in its tattered wrappings after its discovery in 1881 in an abandoned tomb, where it had been placed for safekeeping

In the case of Thutmose I, however, it was discovered that the priests of the Twenty-first Dynasty had made an error in re-bandaging. The mummy labeled Thutmose I turned out to be that of an unknown youth of about eighteen. Thutmose I, who must have been about fifty when he died, has not so far been found.

In 1898, yet another tomb was found in the Valley of the Kings crammed with mummies hidden away for safekeeping by priests. In this group were found Amenhotep II, Thutmose IV, Amenhotep III, Ramses IV, and Ramses V, among others. They, too, were brought to the museum's Mummy Room to be displayed in glass cases.

Little by little the gaps in Egypt's royal history were being filled in. Mummies were being found, and so were the empty, echoing tombs of their onetime owners, magnificent with their painted walls and ceilings but bare of their contents. People wondered if anyone would ever uncover a royal tomb that looked just as it had on the

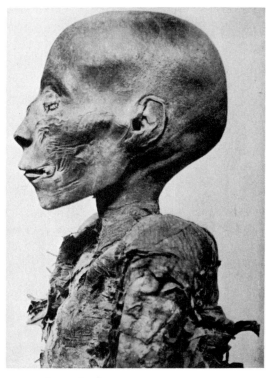

The incorrectly labeled mummy of Thutmose I, later found to be that of an unknown young man

day that the mourners departed and the entrance was sealed, presumably forever.

One such person was a British archaeologist named Howard Carter. He had come to Egypt in 1890 as a very young man and worked there for many years, dreaming constantly of finding an undisturbed tomb in the Valley of the Kings. Digging in the Valley was a costly undertaking, however. So Carter was lucky in having met up with a wealthy British nobleman, Lord Carnarvon, who shared Carter's goal and funded his work.

Because of his health, Lord Carnarvon spent winters in Egypt's warm, dry climate. The months from November to March were also the only time when digging in the Valley was possible. The summers were far too hot.

By 1922, Carter had spent six unsuccessful seasons

fine-combing a particular part of the Valley in search of the burial place of a little-known pharaoh named Tutankhamen. Years earlier another archeologist had discovered some puzzling remains both near and under a large tilted rock in the vicinity. They included a bit of gold leaf and a blue cup marked with Tutankhamen's name. There were also some dried floral collars and some animal bones left behind by the guests of a funeral banquet of long, long ago. Could they have been the guests at the funeral banquet of Tutankhamen?

In the autumn of 1922 Carter arrived in the Valley for what was to be the very last season of the search for Tutankhamen. He brought with him a tiny companion, a canary, to keep him company in the small, domed house he had built for himself on the Valley road on the west bank of the Nile. The local Egyptians hired to work on the dig were amazed by the "golden bird." No songbirds had ever been seen or heard in the grim, treeless Valley.

A painted wooden head of King Tutankhamen as a young boy

Perhaps, as Carter's work team predicted, the little canary brought Carter luck. The site he had chosen for the last season's dig was directly under some ancient grave-workers' huts in front of the tomb of Ramses VI, a pharaoh who had lived about two hundred years later than Tutankhamen. In the past, Carter had hesitated to dig there because the empty tomb of Ramses VI was a heavily visited tourist attraction.

As it turned out, the innocent-appearing workers' huts stood atop none other than the long-forgotten tomb of Tutankhamen. On the very day that the foundations of the first hut were dug away, a step was discovered cut into the rock beneath it. Another step and then another revealed sixteen steps in all. These led down to a sealed passageway filled with broken rocks and then to a second sealed doorway leading into the tomb itself.

Carter sent a historic telegram to Lord Carnarvon who was still in England. It read: "At last have made wonderful discovery in Valley; a magnificent tomb with seals intact; re-covered same for your arrival; congratulations."

On November 26, 1922, with Lord Carnarvon beside him, Carter made an eye-level opening in the door to the tomb and put a candle through the hole. His own words record the thrill of that moment in which he glimpsed the inside of the tomb.

"At first I could see nothing, the hot air escaping from the chamber causing the candle to flicker, but presently, as my eyes grew accustomed to the light, details of the room within emerged slowly from the mist, strange animals, statues, and gold — everywhere the glint of gold. For the moment. . . . I was struck dumb with amaze-

The jumbled treasure in the first room of Tutankhamen's tomb as first seen by Howard Carter

ment, and when Lord Carnarvon, unable to stand the suspense any longer, inquired anxiously, 'Can you see anything?' it was all I could do to get out the words, 'Yes, wonderful things.' "

Carter was looking into the first of four rooms of a surprisingly small royal tomb. The Antechamber, as the first and largest room was called, was only about twelve by twenty-six feet, the measurements of a fair-sized living room. It was heaped with chairs, footstools, and chests of alabaster, ebony, and ivory, and strange couches of gilded wood in the form of animals, including a cow and a lion. Piled beneath the cow-bed were egg-shaped food containers made of clay.

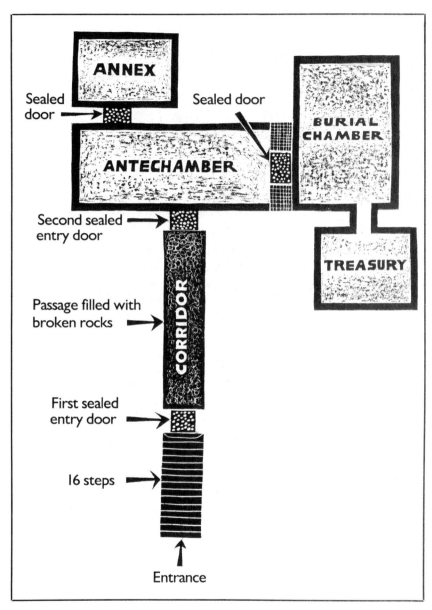

ANNEX

Sealed door

Sealed door

ANTECHAMBER

BURIAL CHAMBER

TREASURY

Second sealed entry door

Passage filled with broken rocks

CORRIDOR

First sealed entry door

16 steps

Entrance

The floor plan of the tomb of Tutankhamen

Sealed doorways, one guarded by two gold-encrusted statues of Tutankhamen, led to the other three rooms of the tomb — an Annex that was even more jumbled than the Antechamber, the Burial Chamber in which the mummy lay, and a small room beyond that called the Treasury.

Carter was not surprised at the disarray that met his eyes, for he had already suspected that Tutankhamen's tomb had been broken into in ancient times. But the robbers had had to leave hastily, even dropping some gold rings and other small articles on their way out. Their lost loot had probably included the bit of gold leaf and the blue cup found outside the tomb in Carter's day. The cemetery officials of ancient times had apparently roughly tidied and resealed the tomb. Then, happily, its entrance had been completely covered over by the building of the Ramses VI workers' huts.

Three anxious and tension-filled years were to pass before the great moment when Carter opened the coffin containing the mummy of Tutankhamen. During that time, while he was carefully cataloging and clearing the contents of the Antechamber, a number of strange events took place.

First, Carter's canary was eaten by a poisonous desert snake. Those who were superstitious took it as a bad omen. Did the snake represent the pharaoh's anger at having had his tomb disturbed? On his death mask, it was later discovered, Tutankhamen wore the cobra and vulture, twin royal symbols of Lower and Upper Egypt.

Next, less than five months after the opening of the tomb, Lord Carnarvon died of blood poisoning from a mysterious insect bite on his cheek that had become infected. He was never to see the great, carved stone coffin in the Burial Chamber that rested inside a series of four nested wooden cases covered with gold leaf. Nor was he ever to see the three richly gleaming mummy-shaped coffins nested inside the rectangular stone coffin or, of course, the mummy of Tutankhamen.

Lastly, soon after the discovery of the tomb, Carter himself ran up against numerous problems with the Egyptian government. One of the disputes had to do with which officials and their guests were to be permitted to visit the tomb while the delicate work of recording its contents was going on. For a time the tomb was sealed up, and Carter actually left Egypt in anger and despair.

Did all of these unpleasant happenings have a hidden meaning? Was there such a thing as a "mummy's curse"? Were Carter and Carnarvon being punished for unearthing the resting place of the pharaoh who had slept longer in his treasure-filled tomb than any other yet known?

Many people thought so. They went to great trouble to try to prove that death was stalking and striking all who had worked with Carter, from the humblest laborer to the most distinguished archaeologist. But Carter himself never believed the wild stories that sprang from his discovery. And, in fact, he went on to live for many more years, dying in 1939 at the age of sixty-five.

The first viewing of Tutankhamen's mummy took place at last in the autumn of 1925. Of the three mummy-shaped coffins, the two outer ones were of wood covered with sheets of gold, while the innermost was of solid gold!

The solid-gold mask found on the mummy of Tutankhamen

Inside the gold innermost coffin lay the bandaged mummy of Tutankhamen, its head and shoulders covered with a solid-gold mask inlaid with blue lapis lazuli, other semi-precious stones, and colored glass. The mask, serene, youthful, and noble, shows the king wearing the ceremonial false beard and a striped headcloth called a *nemes* (NEM-eez) with the royal cobra and vulture at the brow.

The hasty thieves of ancient times who had invaded Tutankhamen's tomb had been looking only for small objects they could carry away quickly. They had entered the Burial Chamber but had never broken into any of its nested coffins.

On unwrapping the mummy, Carter discovered that there were thirteen layers of linen bandages containing one hundred and forty-three precious gold and bejeweled objects. Among them were necklaces, collars, pendants, bracelets, rings, belts, gold-sheathed daggers, gold sandals, and slender golden tubes that encased the mummy's fingernails and toenails.

Beneath all this splendor, however, the mummy itself was a pitiful disappointment. Blackened and shrunken by the careless pouring on of oils and resins, it was one of the poorer examples of the New Kingdom art of mummification.

Who was Tutankhamen? Why was he buried in such a small tomb with such great riches? Why was his mummy so badly prepared?

To Carter's disappointment, no papyrus scrolls telling anything of Tutankhamen's reign or of his family history were found in the tomb. We know only that he is believed to have been either the brother or the illegitimate son of the previous king, Amenhotep IV, who had turned away from the many gods of Thebes to worship the sun as the one and only god. In so doing, Amenhotep IV changed his name to Akhenaten (Ahk-eh-NAH-ten), meaning "pleasing to Aten" (the sun). He also moved his capital from Thebes to a new site known as Akhetaten (Ahk-eh-TAH-ten), or "horizon of the Aten."

Akhenaten, his wife, and daughter worshipping the sun, its rays ending in hands that appear to be blessing them

As Akhenaten's successor, Tutankhamen is thought to have come to the throne as a child of nine, to have reigned briefly, and to have died as a youth of eighteen. He married a princess who may have been his half-sister. He left no heirs. In the richly stocked Treasury, the room just off the Burial Chamber, Carter found two tiny coffins with the mummified remains of girl infants who had probably been dead at birth. Were they the children of Tutankhamen and his young wife?

As to Tutankhamen himself, we do not know how or why he died. Was his death caused by an accident, an illness, or could he have been murdered? There is a suspicious scar, possibly from an arrow tip, in front of the mummy's ear. Did the priests of Thebes who served the many gods want Tutankhamen dead because of his rela-

The outermost gilded wood coffin in which the mummy of King Tutankhamen rests today in the Burial Chamber of his tomb

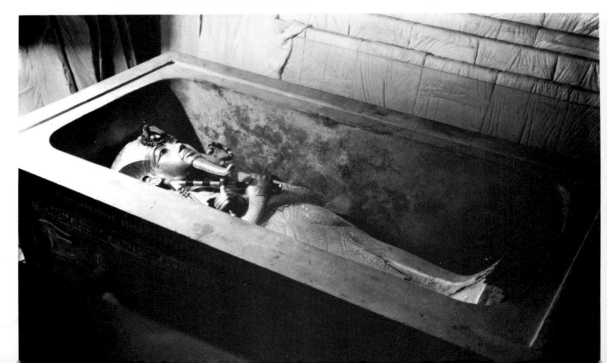

tionship with Akhenaten, who had turned his back on their religion?

Whatever the reason, Tutankhamen's sudden death may account for the small size of his tomb. Perhaps it had been meant for someone else but was used for the young pharaoh because his own was not ready. On the other hand, Tutankhamen may simply have been an unimportant king who, through Howard Carter's discovery, became the most famous of all of Egypt's kings.

If Tutankhamen's treasure, however, was that of an "unimportant" king buried in a hastily prepared tomb, can we ever guess at the splendor of the contents of those much larger and grander tombs that the grave robbers of Egypt emptied thousands of years ago!

The toppled head of Ramses II, among the last of the great conquering pharaohs, lying at the foot of his ruined west bank temple, the Ramesseum

7

The Last of the Mummies

With the last of the pharaohs of the New Kingdom, its glories began to fade. The Egyptian kings had probably overreached themselves with their conquests of foreign lands. Their armies suffered from a lack of iron weapons, and they began to be defeated by their Asian enemies.

The rulers of the Twenty-first Dynasty must have decided it was time for a change. They moved the capital away from Thebes to the flat, watery delta in the far north. This is the part of Egypt where the Nile River empties into the sea. In ancient times, the triangular, or fan-shaped, delta was veined with streams of outflowing water. Today, because of the building of dams, the Nile separates into two main branches that enter the sea at the coastal towns of Rosetta and Damietta.

The new capital was at a place called Tanis. Perhaps the kings wanted their headquarters to be nearer to Egypt's borders for purposes of defense. Another reason for the move may have been that the Nile floodwaters at Thebes had been at a low level for many years. In the delta, there was always water to irrigate the fields, and there was rainfall as well. In this damp, green region it was hard to imagine that most of Egypt was a desert land.

There was one problem, though. There was no way to dig underground shafts leading to deep burial chambers in the soggy soil of the delta. If you dug a really deep hole, it soon filled up with water. And moisture was the known enemy of all mummies.

So the kings of Tanis had themselves buried in shallow stone chambers under the floors of their temples. The aboveground temples, however, crumbled long ago. Many were destroyed by invaders who knew nothing of the tombs that lay just beneath the muddied stone foundations.

It was not until 1939 that archaeologists digging in the delta began to find the burial chambers of the Tanis kings. Many had been looted in ancient times. But some were filled with treasure almost as rich as that of Tutankhamen. There were solid silver coffins, gold and silver cups and bowls, gold masks, gold sandals, gold toe and finger sheaths, and jeweled charms to ensure the mummy's passage into the afterlife.

Even though the capital of Egypt had been moved to the delta starting with the Twenty-first Dynasty, Thebes continued to be an important city. It was the center of worship of the god Amen-Ra and was ruled by a powerful priesthood. In keeping with religious practice, the Egyptians went on making mummies at Thebes and throughout the kingdom. Some were very well preserved.

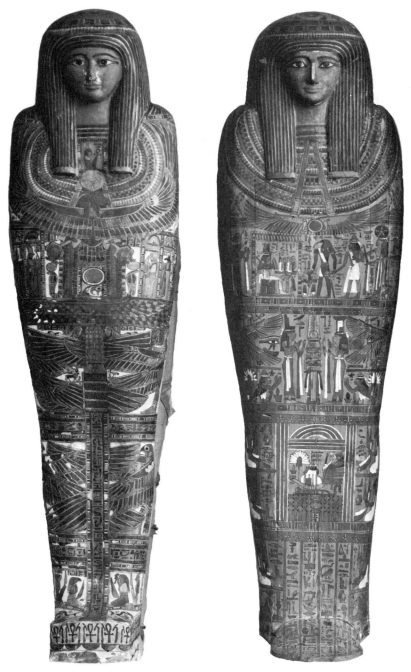

Painted wood mummy cases of the 22nd Dynasty, part of a set of three nested coffins, found at Thebes and containing the mummy of a priest of Amen-Ra. The feather patterns represent the sheltering wings of the goddesses Isis and Nephthys.

99

Others, like those of Tanis, showed early signs of decay because of the damp delta climate. Still others were poorly prepared, but their partially rotted bodies were hidden in elaborately painted mummy cases or under gorgeous and showy wrappings.

There was also a growing trend toward a kind of "assembly-line" mummy-making. The seventy-day preparation with its long drying-out period on a bed of natron was too slow and costly for many people. Also, the oils and resins, which came mainly from Asia, grew scarce and expensive as the Egyptian empire shrank.

There was a new demand for "instant" mummification. And this was arranged by dipping the bodies in black, tarry pitch, or asphalt, a substance similar to that used today for coating roads and driveways. The pitch dried the body quickly to rocklike hardness.

How did the Egyptians, with their deep honor and respect for tradition, take to these changes? The answer is, partly, that many of the kings and their people were no longer Egyptian. Between the Twenty-second and the Thirtieth Dynasty, most of Egypt's kings were of foreign birth. Among them were Libyans and Nubians from Africa, followed by Assyrians and Persians from Asia. Finally, after the Thirtieth Dynasty, there were Greeks and Romans from Europe.

The Greeks, under the famed general Alexander the Great, conquered Egypt in 332 B.C. Alexander founded the bustling, worldly city of Alexandria on the northern coast of Egypt. Greek rule in Egypt lasted for three hundred years, ending with the well-known queen Cleopatra.

Mummification was unknown to the Greeks. Their custom had been to burn the bodies of the dead. But they soon adopted the Egyptian practice of mummification. Even Alexander the Great was mummified. His body is said to be lying to this day somewhere beneath the busy sidewalks of Alexandria.

The Greeks, who in their own religion worshipped many gods, began also to worship the gods of Egypt. They even built temples to them along the Nile, at places like Dendera, Edfu, Kom Obo, and in Nubia, that were more like the earlier Egyptian temples than like any Greek temples. And they continued the worship of the Apis bull, mummifying many of the huge animals just as the Egyptians had done for centuries.

The Romans followed the Greeks as rulers of Egypt. They, too, took on the Egyptian custom of mummifying their dead. They then buried them in underground tombs, which they called catacombs.

A Greek-made statue of the Egyptian goddess Isis that once stood in Alexandria

An elaborately wrapped mummy of a boy of Roman times in Egypt, wearing a painted portrait mask

In Alexandria, the catacombs of the wealthy Romans can still be visited today. They are carved out of solid rock and lie a hundred feet beneath the city pavements, at the bottom of a long spiral staircase. About three hundred tombs are arranged on three levels. Some are mere niches in the walls, while others are larger burial chambers. The size of the Roman mummy's tomb depended on what the family could afford or how important the person was.

Some of the dead in the Alexandria catacombs had already become Christians, members of the new religion based on the teachings of Jesus Christ. The linen bandages in which their mummies were wrapped were marked with a cross on the forehead. Although the Christian religion was to forbid the mummification of the dead, some Christians in Egypt continued to practice mummification up to about six hundred years after the death of Christ.

During the time of Roman rule and the early years of Christianity, many changes in the old burial customs took place in Egypt. Strange religious carvings appeared in tombs and temples, showing that people were out of touch with the past.

In the Alexandria catacombs, wall reliefs show three canopic jars instead of the traditional four. A funeral banquet is pictured, but it takes place in a typical Roman dining room. And the god Anubis appears as a male figure with the head of a jackal, but he is dressed in a Roman military uniform!

Meantime, out in the public square of Alexandria, an Egyptian sphinx wearing the *nemes* — the headdress

An Egyptian sphinx in Alexandria with the cross of the Christian religion carved on its forehead

worn by Egyptian kings from Khafre to Tutankhamen — is seen to have a Christian cross carved on its forehead. Oddly, though, the cross is made up of four loops, recalling the looped top of the ancient Egyptian ankh, the sign for life.

The most sweeping change of all, however, for Egypt, its ancient gods, and its mummies, came in the year 640 with the introduction of the brand-new religion of Islam. This powerful faith, meaning "submission" (to the will of God), had arisen only a short time earlier in Arabia, an Asian peninsula that lay close to Egypt. The founder of Islam was a preacher and prophet named Mohammed, and its followers were called Moslems.

The Moslems believed in one god only. Under Islam there were to be no more mummies, no more gods of the dead, no more charms or provisions for the afterlife, no more painted tomb walls, and no more carved stone temples to Ra, Isis, Horus, or any other god of the old religion. The new Moslem cemeteries contained simple graves. Most were in low, aboveground structures. Some had small domes that distantly resembled the ones atop the mosques, or Moslem houses of worship. The bodies laid in them were merely washed and buried quickly after death. The preservation of the body was not considered essential to the survival of the soul.

The city of Cairo, built by the Moslems, became the new capital of Egypt. In a fairly short time, most Egyptians became Moslems. The new religion changed their language to Arabic, the language in which the Koran, or holy book of Islam, was written. Soon, Egypt's hieroglyphic language and its ancient religion had passed from the scene. And its mummies, too, had been forgotten. Or had they?

One of the strangest fates of all awaited the mummies of ancient Egypt. Some time around the year 1000, people in Europe began to get the idea that dried mummies had miraculous healing powers. Perhaps this was because they were so long-lasting. But there seems to be another reason.

For a long time, Europeans had used a curative powder that was made from a dark, pitch-like substance called bitumen. Bitumen oozed out of cracks in the rocks of certain mountains in distant Persia. When it hardened it was ground into fine particles that could be swallowed or placed on sores and wounds.

The problem, however, was that bitumen from Persia was scarce and very costly. Egyptian mummies that had been dipped in pitch were dark and brittle. Perhaps they contained the bitumen that everyone was seeking. Astonishingly, a new trade sprang up. Hundreds of thousands of mummies were dug up, most of them from the common pits where the hastily mummified poor had been buried. Their bodies, whole or in parts, were then shipped off to the apothecaries, or drug merchants, of Europe, where they were ground to powder!

What was ground-up mummy thought to be good for? Almost everything. It was taken by mouth as a remedy for concussions, paralysis, epilepsy, ulcers, coughs, headaches, and poisoning. It was also applied to bruises and broken bones, and it was said to stop bleeding and prevent infection. King Francis I, who ruled France in the 1500s, never went anywhere without his pouch of ground mummy just in case he fell off his horse or had some other unexpected injury.

Did ground mummy really contain any bitumen? And did bitumen itself have any true medicinal value? People believed that bitumen did cure many ills and that Egypt's mummies contained it. Pitch and bitumen are very similar chemically, so people may have been right about the so-called benefits of bitumen being found in mummy. In fact, the very word *mummy* has come to us from the Persian word *mūm* and the Arabic word *mūmiyah*, both of which mean bitumen. In any case, the demand for dried mummy went on and on for hundreds of years.

By the 1600s, so many ancient Egyptian grave pits had been emptied that there wasn't enough ground-mummy medicine to go around. A grisly new trade sprang up. The bodies of criminals, beggars, disease victims, and other newly dead were manufactured into "instant" mummies by dipping them in pitch or asphalt and letting them dry quickly in the sun. Even the bodies of animals were said to have been used for this purpose.

Little by little the news of the mummy "factories" and the trickery of the mummy traders leaked out. People began to realize how foolish they had been. They drew back in horror and, during the 1700s, the demand for ground mummy started to drop off.

But the mummy manufacturers hated to lose their business. They continued to make instant ground mummy, and they sold it as bone meal and fertilizer to British farmers. Ground mummy was also used as an ingredient in mixing artists' paints. Perhaps some believed that the powder would help the colors — or even the works of art themselves — to last.

Even the torn, discolored linen wrappings stripped from the ancient Egyptian mummies were sold abroad. In the 1800s, paper mills in the United States bought them as rags to use in papermaking. But, as a mill in Maine soon discovered, the resin-soaked bandages were hard to bleach white, so they had to be used for making brown paper. In Egypt, the linen bandages of the mummies had long been used by the poor for fuel because the resin in them burned well.

With all the terrible destruction of the mummies over the years, it's a wonder that there are any left today. Compared with the millions — possibly hundreds of millions—of mummies that were made in Egypt, the number of those that have survived is indeed very small.

Fortunately, we now realize how rare and valuable the mummies that are left to us are. With the help of modern medicine and X-ray techniques, we are now caring for the mummies in new ways and learning more about them than ever before.

The mummy of King Seti I, now carefully preserved in Cairo

Taking measurements of the mummies has told us that most Egyptians were of slender build and short to medium height, about five to five-and-a-half feet tall. Almost none were fat.

X-rays tell us much more. Bone development reveals a person's age. So we now know that the average life-span of the ancient Egyptians was about forty. King Ramses II, however, was an exception. He is believed to have lived to the age of ninety. His height, too, was above average, for he was six feet tall.

X-raying the mummies' bones also tells us that they suffered from arthritis and other bone deformities. Their feet, though, were generally healthy, for they didn't cramp them into tight shoes. Even the pharaohs wore sandals of soft leather or woven papyrus, or simply went barefoot.

The Egyptians had no sugar. Honey was their only sweetener and they probably never developed a "sweet tooth." So they had very little tooth decay. But their teeth were worn down almost to the gums, even in the mummies of those who had died quite young. Researchers think this is because the Egyptians' bread, an important part of their diet, had a lot of sand and grit in it. This was due to the stone tools used in reaping and grinding the grain. Fine bits of the stone rubbed or chipped off and got into the flour from which the bread was baked.

Some of the diseases the ancient Egyptians had are still around today in Egypt. One of them is bilharziasis (bill-hahr-ZI-uh-sis). It's caused by a parasite carried by snails that live in the stagnant water of the irrigation canals.

A towering statue of King Ramses II at the Temple of Karnak. The carved figure of his wife is much smaller to indicate her lesser importance.

The parasite pierces the skin of those who go barefoot in the waterlogged fields or bathe in the canals. Once the parasite enters the bloodstream, it can damage the bladder and other organs, leading to loss of blood and even death. Amazingly, the mummy of a youth of ancient Egypt and the body of an Egyptian peasant boy of today can show symptoms of having been attacked by the same species of "bug."

In recent times, the mummies in the Mummy Room of the Cairo Museum have had to be treated for both old and new fungus infections. After resting for thousands of years in the dry heat of their desert tombs, they were moved to Cairo, where they did not react well to the changes in climate and air quality. Even inside their sealed glass cases, many suffered from the increased dampness and from being breathed on by too many visitors.

The mummy of Ramses II was in especially bad shape. It had been attacked by many kinds of fungi, bacteria, and insects. So, in 1976 it was carefully shipped to France where it was X-rayed, analyzed, and treated. After seven months, it was pronounced cured and was sterilized against further decay. It was then shipped back to Egypt with great fanfare.

Ramses II, who lived over three thousand years ago, was king for sixty-seven years and left more monuments to himself all over Egypt than any other ruler. His immense portraits in stone ranged from the delta in the north to Abu Simbel in the south. He would probably have been very proud of all the special treatment lavished on him so long after his death.

Four stone portraits of Ramses II, over 65 feet high, fronting his famous temple at Abu Simbel in southern Egypt

An Egyptian tomb painting of musicians and dancers entertaining at a banquet. The artist's work reveals a love of life that we are invited to share with those who lived in the distant past.

Did the mummified dead of ancient Egypt "live for ever," as they so desperately wanted to? In some way, they did.

In carrying out their preparations for death, the ancient Egyptians managed to preserve an indelible picture of the Egyptian way of life. No other people of the past has left us such a lively and intimate record of a world that existed over five thousand years ago.

We look at their painted tomb walls and we see their joy in music and dancing, their pleasure in the world of nature, their delight in beauty of every kind.

Perhaps, then, the true role of the mummies was to link the past with the present, and to share with us the life they loved so much that they wanted it never to end.

Bibliography

Aldred, Cyril, *Egypt to the End of the Old Kingdom.* London: Thames and Hudson, 1965. Reprint. N.Y.: Thames and Hudson, 1982.

Brackman, Arnold C., *The Search for the Gold of Tutankhamen.* N.Y.: Mason-Charter, 1976. Reprint. N.Y.: Pocket, 1977.

Carter, Howard and Mace, A. C., *The Tomb of Tut*Ankh* Amen Discovered by the Late Earl of Carnarvon and Howard Carter.* London: Cassell and Company Ltd.; Volume I, 1923; Volume II, 1927; Volume III, 1933. Abridged three-volume version. *The Tomb of Tutankhamen.* N.Y.: Dutton, 1972. Reprint Volume I. *The Discovery of the Tomb of Tutankhamen.* N.Y.: Dover, 1977.

Desroches-Noblecourt, Christiane, *Tutankhamen: Life and Death of a Pharaoh.* London: Michael Joseph Ltd., 1963. First American edition. N.Y.: New York Graphic Society, 1963.

Edwards, Amelia B., *A Thousand Miles Up the Nile.* London: Century Publishing, Ltd., 1982. First published in Great Britain by Longmans, 1877.

Edwards, I.E.S., *The Treasures of Tutankhamun.* London: Michael Joseph Ltd., 1972. First American edition. N.Y.: Viking, 1973. Reprint. N.Y.: Penguin, 1976.

Glubok, Shirley and Tamarin, Alfred, *The Mummy of Ramose: The Life and Death of an Ancient Egyptian Nobleman.* N.Y.: Harper and Row, 1978.

Hamilton-Paterson, James and Andrews, Carol, *Mummies: Death and Life in Ancient Egypt.* N.Y.: Viking, 1979.

Hoving, Thomas, *Tutankhamun: The Untold Story.* N.Y.: Simon and Schuster, 1978.

Hutchinson, Warner A., *Ancient Egypt: Three Thousand Years of Splendor.* N.Y.: Grosset and Dunlap, 1978.

James, T.G.H., *The Archeology of Ancient Egypt.* N.Y.: Walck, 1972.

Leca, Ange-Pierre, *The Egyptian Way of Death: Mummies and the Cult of the Immortal.* Paris: Hachette, 1976. First American Edition. Garden City, N.Y.: Doubleday, 1981.

Lurker, Manfred, *The Gods and Symbols of Ancient Egypt: An Illustrated Dictionary.* German edition. Otto Wilhelm Barth, 1974. First British edition. London: Thames and Hudson, 1980. Reprint. N.Y.: Thames and Hudson, 1984.

McHargue, Georgess, *Mummies.* Philadelphia and N.Y.: Lippincott, 1972.

Mertz, Barbara, *Red Land, Black Land: Daily Life in Ancient Egypt.* N.Y.: Dodd, Mead & Co., 1966. Revised edition. N.Y.: Dodd, Mead & Co., 1978.

————, *Temples, Tombs, and Hieroglyphs: A Popular History of Ancient Egypt.* N.Y.: Dodd, Mead & Co., 1964. Revised edition. N.Y.: Dodd, Mead & Co., 1978.

Pace, Mildred Mastin, *Wrapped for Eternity: The Story of the Egyptian Mummy.* N.Y.: McGraw-Hill, 1974.

Romer, John, *People of the Nile: Everyday Life in Ancient Egypt.* First American edition. N.Y.: Crown, 1982.

Spencer, A. J., *Death in Ancient Egypt.* London: Penguin, 1982.

Vandenberg, Philipp, *The Golden Pharaoh.* German edition. C. Bertelsmann, 1978. First American edition. N.Y.: Macmillan, 1980.

White, Jon Manchip, *Everyday Life in Ancient Egypt.* N.Y.: Putnam, 1963.

Index